forgiveness is a disappearing act

nikolina lazetic

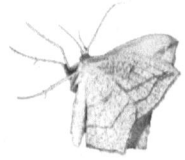

Spuyten Duyvil
New York City

acknowledgements

thank you to all who, along the way, made language possible:

to Julie, for the raw beauty without which this book would not exist;
to Mónica and EG—the luminous ones;
to Marina, my sister, an anchor and inspiration throughout;
to my MFA cohort at Brown and those there who nourished the pages; for the art, another world;
to the woman I used to call "my little winner," who already knows;
to Luke, for the off-road magic and unconditional support; hands;
to my friends here, now;
to friends and family in Sarajevo, some no longer of this world;
to Sarajevo;
to Aurelia, Tod, Spuyten Duyvil for accepting and allowing the hybrid wings to unfurl;
to all other Others, for the silences.

an early portion of this book was composed in response to and read (performed) in collaboration with/alongside dancer, artist and scholar Julie Dind. her rhythm lingers, shines.

©Nikolina Lazetic
ISBN 978-1-952419-96-6

Library of Congress Control Number: 2021941809

the *I* of this book is a pendulum. like every story, this is a love story. there is no end; the end is everywhere.

everyone has wet thoughts about mute Salome

          in the etymological sense *I*
    am   discrete quantities
              of energy,   rhythm
              preceding evidence,
           the air of song beneath
             gender or the edge of
         a spell capable of drawing
    blood,   in thin lines.

I.

the sum of shadows you cast equals the weight of light.
stone by stone, a shore articulates the river of oblivion.

"hunger can be hard to recognize," I read on a billboard seconds before the roadkill and I feel awkwardly *seen*, then nauseated. my hands retrieve the feeling of a small bird the dog had killed in the yard a few nights ago and I held for too long, mesmerized by a hollow softness.
memory of touch can feel no different than the touch.

the I, I should remind me, is fiction. *you are not just a suicide waiting to happen.*

you lose someone, and somebody asks if *you feel like a part is missing, do you feel like an amputee.* your smile as you answer *no, my whole being is a phantom limb.* you feel absent in an angelic sense: a common bird winging its way through knotted time, its god being a blind terminal.

think of everything that can break in a human; write it down, and it does.

when a bird, blinded by the reflection, crashes into a window, body leaves an imprint. the bird dies on impact, and the soft cellophane of oil forms a near-invisible geometry, akin to a cobweb or slipknot. chipped wings become a dying alphabet.

my sister calls to tell me we are addicted to leaving, and that I need to fight my addiction. sure, I say, aware of my tone's anemia. *I am not trying to tell you how to live your life, I'm telling you to live it.*

at some point, the difference between the cage and a lung is negligible.

once, I saw a woman carry a glass of milk to a site of explosion; she was too poor to afford flowers. not long after, I had a dream of several uniformed men stretching a canvas out of this glass.

In 2001, during an early sunrise a naked woman is seen hula hooping at a beach between Jaffa and Tel Aviv. the hoop is barbed wire and, torn between the symptom and cause, she hollows where there is flesh; after two minutes, her abdomen is smears of nacre and rose silica. the woman's name is Sigalit Landau.

a wound is not a regret.

walking the pinkblack acres, I gather bird bones offered by a dry earth; I name her Sylvia, meaning *of the woods*. enumerate your losses by the steps you take, I think to myself, and see what else in this world you're afraid of. funny how often we forget our bodies are just bare facts of the ground.

that, and how there's never a real lack of strangers' funerals to attend.

a train zooms by and I feel alive, or, at least not severed from the wind. for a moment inside a mild and analogue weather, I am no longer bound to the prospect of disappearing. a train zooms by and the wings gulp, then void the winds.
millions of dust particles away from the thinking part of me, I watch my shadow empty the sun: a brief intelligence begging release.

in a dream, eyes of the prophets are all apples; god cuts them straight through. of god, I see the back: wind-colored, coiled miracle—a compass gone out of breath.

against the concrete-gray sky, pale fuchsia of a carcass is dotting the edge of the field and decomposing into monosyllables, crumbs of eucharist.

the psychosis of every moment is its simultaneity with my body: every cell stores a memory of irretrievable hands, dimmed intimacy, different parts of bleeding. yearnings piled up like an atheist's rosaries.

I meet someone at a bar, and, after a few drinks, say *I often imagine a knife, or, more a dagger-type instrument, sliding just under this large birthmark on my chest. I imagine it in slow-motion and in detail—myself, alone with a slender elegance and the red announcement, exposed to the bedroom light and submerged, extreme touch.* mid-sentence I watch my whole body surround him; an halation, nightnothing. the edge of his wineglass bristles with incandescent dew; I catch a whiff of magnolia, hibiscus, pale romanticism. his eyes on me are the slippery skins of grapes as he says something like *you look like the light before light, like leaving,* as I think up the ways a woman is likely to disappear.

sit in the middle of the senses and wait for something to give, I whisper to myself, *appalachia, wolf sightings*—I try to take my mind off the moment, remembering the mesh of a tent and discarded snakeskin outstretched in the cold neon of morning light.

later, he shows me how glass is blown; flame stiffens into folds of light. I then watch him break what are considered to be the failed forms and feel the blood rush to my head, say *do you not know a butterfly with a broken wing can still fly* and *how can you be sure the pieces of the mirror you're throwing out are empty.*

facts settle into parts of the body. I can put my hand on the exact place where I feel time come to an end.

when I hear my dead speak, I imagine pieces of earth falling through the cracks in their lips. mouths so dry you could pluck black petals out of every word.

it could take a lifetime to tell a single silence.

one kept memory of home is grandmother asking that I lend my eyes to the box of remained Yugoslav coins, her voice stretched too thin. sunlight turns her wrinkled hands into coils of
burnt linen.
this isn't about the living, this currency.

what I mean to say is, when I was little, grandma comforted me: in the dark, anyone could be a refugee.

an angel is one punishable flaw you can find in a darkness.
imagine the endless going on about a winged and flightless
business of unconditional love, unable to partake of any. being
angel, you swim through water that refuses to touch you. as in—
you're washing the world's water clean and you're dying of thirst.
picture just how hellish 'angelic' rage must be.

a woman is walking down Sarajevo's sniper alley, naked. she covers
her breasts with her hands and a male voice warns her that hands are
not allowed; she drops them and continues to walk, looking down,
serpentine arms coiled by the sides of her body.
on the other side of the dream, I am holding a freshly chopped 7-year-
long braid in my arms, crying: this is the day I go to the embassy.
this would be my first visa interview.

mid-night, the silk caressing my form spills into clefs of light; in any
moment, a lightning somewhere is enveloping the desert. the desert
is beginning to resemble a river—a former country divulging into
former water.
what does it mean to be a nomad without a people?

two things I know how: withhold words like no other and hold my
hunger for a while.
two things I know: love is everything and love is never enough.

my apartment brims with marrow and incense. a few paintings—mostly movement captures, distortions of light through texture—line the edges of the floors, bruise-colored blends of acrylic and pastel. rows of century-old postcards I use as canvases lean out of the walls, teeth-like; below them are candles in repurposed jam-jars, a semblance of cracked eggshells I call archangels. shelves and the desk are home to two cat skulls and a few rodent spines, bird pelvic bone, one deer antler with thorns sticking out of it—found sacrifices I'd made bloodless in soap and peroxide. I take photographs of un-mourned roadkill: this is how I contextualize my losses.
I am writing this so I wouldn't have to speak. my voice is inconsistent, a body of water torn open by the bora; this place is a salt prison holding it together. an image so grainy there's no demand to tell fact from fiction.

from the window, you can see a large sign spelling "ROSES." the sign registers as a voice coming from a pain, like the word 'pain' that's already a failed prospect as it cannot possibly transmit that which it carries. a word that is plane of tilted agency.

mental illness is like war, it always wins, I scribbled on a post-it resting to the left of the door, thinking it funny. when I look at it, it speaks Akhmatova's words—"you do not know what you were forgiven."

a document is always barbarism. a story, then, is a fugitive form caught at the cusp of captivity.
there is no alibi for a storyteller.

on sleepless nights, I'm dreaming up a story of Rasputin's illegitimate daughter. writing it down, I think only how the morale of this story—my story—should be that what happens to the wolf happens to the people. how, when it comes to love, language is always posthumous.

words, like wolves, are pack animals. hunted, they will haunt you through the night.

I knew a woman who could read fortune from discarded snakeskins. she once placed the skin in my hand and combed through the contortions, saying "see how the light weaves through these parts; this, only women can see." these are the feral glyphs of the ground.

that which does not lack specificity at all lacks magic entirely.

one day you'll feed your last coat to the winds, baby, I tell myself
in her voice, the kind that still registers as touch, as the missing
quieting. the way she says "baby" discolors anger and makes my
skin tighten until I feel transparent.

she exists between time and me, lining the inner edges of my body
and counting up its consequences—something like a closed circuit,
or, *u isto vreme dva zaborava.*

on bad days, she'd bring out a box of nesting dolls she had drawn
character t-shirts on; *I'm going to unpack your anger,* she'd say while
pulling the matryoshkas, one by one, out. her hands teach me that
nudity can mean more than a site of destruction.

nothing in this world is meant to exist as a comparison; not even a
naked rock.

we're wishbones broken for someone else's good luck, she said, now a while ago, *and wishbones aren't even human bones so, really, nothing to be sad about.* perhaps a wishbone does not snap but disperses into magnetized weapons—a thing akin to coilguns, ion or plasma cannons.

water retains its shape inside a layered rock, and, when heated, causes the rock to contract and expand. this, then, may cause the rock to explode. this, also, is how missing her works.

If water got bruised, how would you tell I tend to ask out of an impulse to say anything, to silence the thoughts I know better than to externalize. thinking, really, *how the fuck do you go on like this.*

I am thirsty but there's a desert at the bottom of the river
sister I am thirsty for the water from the bottom of the river

where I am from, blood is always a promise. someone in my research seminar says *a thought does not bleed* and I say *try me*, then don't say anything for the rest of the semester.
I think of an essayist as a person who collects roadkill.

my sister's endometriosis means she bleeds for months at a time and no one can explain how.
I learned to live with not knowing you, with never having known you, she calls to tell me, *but it is time you made a home. what I'm telling you to do, it's breaking bones.* I make a bad joke, *baby I'm like a revolution and spread by contamination;* my head is heavy with synth swells of the Levant and the hum of crushed velvet.
I worry about your elegant ribs, she continues, *the winds are blowing up god and you go around flaunting what he'd bestowed.*

In 1974, H.R. Giger presents his painting of herself, Li I, to Li Tobler; she breaks the frame and tears at it. Three years later, Li Tobler will shoot herself in bed; the painting will have been reconstructed since, and the contours of her face can now be traced in almost every one of his works.

tell me: what do *you* do when the only person able to reach you is gone.

in the dream, I am departing someplace and the sky is a mass grave: birds lie open-throated and open-lunged, afloat in an infection. neon-lit signs tell me that it takes 7hr 34 min to get to from Paris to Lyon. I also learn that it takes 11hrs 24min to reach Nova Gorica from Berlin; 15hr 54min Sarajevo. 16hr 19min to walk the length of the Berlin Wall.
although nowhere near unimaginable, some are not the distances we were ever likely to cross.

my abdomen hurts because of the way I say "yes" to people.

the protocol for training Nazi soldiers, I'm told, involved German Shepherds. the men were each given a puppy to raise, teach and train. upon the dogs' reaching adulthood and peak of loyalty, each trainee was instructed to shoot his own.

this is how you sacrifice the true to some truth.

there is black cloth nailed onto the stone walls of houses along the shores of Crkvenica, in Herzegovina. this is a mark of misfortune, of something becoming chipped in a household. it was not unusual to see the black cloth where a woman had been ruled a sinner, most times a witch or an adulteress. here, they'd pulled daughters by their hair from mothers and tore - not hair, not the black veils, but muscle tissue and bone fragments. tongues.
we're taught to count our dead among the living.

when I close my eyes, boats are leaving the dead of winter, and I watch. my father tells me this is the time and place of sun's rebirth so I learn to adore it. my hair catches the smell of smoke; nights, I dream of a lit-up village and snows catching on.
when I try to sleep, I am startled awake by a sound I cannot locate; glass shatters where I cannot reach.

each day I walk past a weathered sculpture of a child in a yard down the street; some days there's also a little girl. the girl and the wood: one and the same, a self in two worlds.
at some point in the story, girl with the velvet hood becomes a wolf. picture a girl as real as the wolf.
I see the little girl behind the wooden child and think *I am approximating myself from a distance now, I am a velvet desert away. I am waiting for the myth to draw breath and for the wood to blossom.*

body is water. war.

my hands fit around my waist and I feel contained; a thing finished and, for a moment, *kept.*

I think I can hear the water crack.

the night I watched the firespinners
the night spun   grief

II.

improvisation is an appeal to the authority of tradition.
I only need a tongue to coat the words with.

may   this body be
the first decision I make.
          body being
     the first. Incision,
     body being. makes
man mad   to look upon

twice the light slit her aborigine, light's abortion. twice the light slid through and knotted. tongue, by any other name. twice the weight of numbers.
 a story only hips remember. charcoal contours, falernum. recount what reeks of amber. Flown

                  I crave an
          incantatory release, to
            sweat   effortless
          shards of glass; long
              to light up this
               city — sniper
having been its cruelest
    month — site-specific
            longing. procure
        sepulcher the structure
                    of silk

ninthnight I don't sleep but watch the fireflies unloosen the glass of spun spit, spines snapped off god's seamless vision — simple improvisation of the self's given points: marrow, clavicle, trembling melee, a moving image of thought without words. little by little these chipped hours unspool black glitter, listen: this is the only way to love. like exile, love is a state of recollecting light

dazzled   teeth
conceal an   obvious
moan, moan   with me: language is lack of enforcement, a
dream of places beyond haunt:
the   back   of   Poland,
         a tyranny of red
flowers, rags of rages; Sarajevska magla, med and mercury; neon sun all flared up inside the cool blast of   bombsight blue, conventional.   pain is an early spirit lengthening world

no David don't / you /
no Ruth I / crave a near-
est seclusion, at last my
body crushed by   veils
of sewed pearls: crumbs
of eucharist, conglomerates of
salt   cleaving, knotted,
ancestral against   being
forgiven.   the light never
touches   anything
          on its way back.
       what I miss I sabotage:
rub   your wrist against my
navel   — look how the roses
wreck the air

to touch a veil
is touching
touch itself, to touch
everything. I touch
myself and let the ghosts pass
through unscathed, un-
spool the gossamer of dry
light. in your arms I'll be
your arms, be scent of
a masochist —
a blade alone with night

nightlong minerva's owl crashes a blind spot, scatters the broken-backed roses — agents of broken crayon — along the rubble of a bombed-out city. I pray that the wing-beat snapped against the winter sun—a sedated moon—be some holy indelible anemic who's come now gushing in

a prayer is　　　　　weightless
holder of hands.　　　what I
touch I weaponize, count up the
evening's earnings: dew un-mirror-
ing rains, a dozen sequestered jew-
els, grains of polystyrene snow, one
towel freshly laundered; pebbles.
not every lamb is sacrificial,
　　　　　　　　　　some starve

if I could I'd let nothing new begin. I'd be the bow underwriting reasonable winds, commanding views; I am the holding on hold. I'd offer a clean bow, halved apples to the halved gods, gods who know fear. I use my body as a relational space, induced openness, dance for *Dodola,* the goddess of rain; I pray she'd rearrange slow-running water, let us plow.   friable river

everything in the brain
is a variable, composition
in erasure; grayscale and
compartmentalized awe.
   we move in efforts
  to intercept our own
 image, invent new inter-
vals to dispel the impro-
vised habit. we move like
laughter, receive
and give our bodies as
   sites of destruction

orllarnent blew up my origin arrcl I exist withil'l quotation marks, skindrum thrown into a wrollg long iin"ervcl between BREATH and delegation,Rnedite'!anean aWE and teške bOje, boje se ne boje and moon blew up the high street likd CICADA congregation. this chrorrology of shit happelli'g allJ'er shit happells still cant explain what violence expelled lls, explode the excuse up holding hisllry in ob)iviorl and Jrright bound in bRead sus'endecl over WATER. everyone standng up wJll their voices trimmed candlls, vigil dropped floor

the image of freedom forms
a running mistranslation
of an anonymous decision.
I name a color any
color and call it Red, *selah:*
I'm dubbing ceasefire
agreement, corrective point.
whereas I speak so as to
remember oblivion, history
is misnomer for canceled
presents

my lips move. think how
a thing so wet is also full
of blood, think of starved
anemones, the word for
sister already slivered. my
how the whales coalesce into
a skeletal rosebud, forming
a dozen new ecosystems. caught
in a nonaligned dream's man-
ic waterways, hiatus forms the
diameters of feeling's field force:
I look as if my whole body had
been crying

the skin on the surface of
milk rises, a semblance of lu-
cid dream or wet not-yet
wake, meat peeled off
snakeskin. webbed in
what hasn't happened yet and
is, what hasn't yet remained
and bleeds spools of not-
yet, still remains too close to
say while speaking, stay—I
want to touch you, un-
break so time falls deaf,
dead. my rivers move
in both directions, there's
nowhere to go but deepen.
maybe you'll hold me, or
time will hold me to you: it's
time my arms came off
 impoverished

                    in her exilic
condition, a moth is by eyesight
bound to the thing   that kills. I
feel usurped and am called *elegant,*
sexy. I adore anything that fucks
me up even halftime, like   lost
happiness, your texts: breath
breaking silhouettes of blown ros-
es. my asylum's   sweet alyssum
        swept

a bridge is   rigid water.
the truth of the bridge is the
truth of the border: mešam lati-
nicu i —cirilicu. as in: I tried
            to speak. my tongue
is a domestic predator.   as
in: I'm told the words I can-
not feel, keep repeating:
rhubarb,   lanugo,
            petrichor

the bridge:

as if
the whole
    world &
        never I
throughout. would
        the fissure and
this
  exigent
take
  the stuttered
in proportion. damn,
        says I, my
delicate
  ee, how how?
ah pretty
        tear, as in
not so. not so
just yet. leave
    leave, take
you with me,
        apart
just so
    enough
atremble. oh so. oh
        so and
    shook
a bullet,
sweat. surmise
    impress
below the all. please
        the weight
        the weight of word

to the bridge:

there are / ways / to impress giants.

you / burn me. the sky / looks nice to / day where I am / not.

for / everything I / have reasons. my reasons / frighten me.

scrub that want   off my
amateur,   resin of
water.   encroachment.
vengeance of words on the
move,   move
-ment generates   theory,
long-legged and   long out
of nationalist unction. broke
       tongue over toothing
-stone.   hymen and out
             -side of hurt

remind me: war doesn't come out of speakers, that's only the river, muffled - mesh sound & thick with gum, algae. locate me against or aghast the tidal reticence, alleviating drowned sands. I hear *she float in beauty* she's trains exploding. I worry about celestial anything blowing up, this collapsible exactitude of my collarbone, all who survived. ravishing a sincere sense of wonder breaks the bonds of social context and frontline methodology. do you remember the *time* our throats smelled of river substrates and ashes in the open sea, night jasmine, shards of runaway glass. even our eyes were a handful, bold objects, aquiline. *can you recall now* wild lungs and socialism: conveyable temperature of light

the voices   of the
thread return to me as   liq-
uid forms   moving in con-
junction. I acknowledge only
the accuracy of feeling,   say-
ings   in Occitan, what in-
undates a tender aura. I wish
for the ability to make a good
thing happen by means of pre-
cise longing. on Earth we are
capable of light, of dispatching
d i s t a n c e s

a shadow set in motion begs the light without. I keep my blades sheathed in petals. of home, I'd kept the canned photocopy ash; I chant to summon the draught and drift by light insured. there is no clemency in slow language, just displaced time

sister I
want to be a bullet and chose　　　　not to kill

swathed in kleptomania-cal tenderness and lapidary tremor, my hips shimmy in semblance of the suspended silver of a photographic image, a little like shadow shedding skin. my sexed body is hypercaptive: breaks down the regime of words consider beauty a reverse exile: god if god were scissors and not a loaned onliness. consider how none among us has seen herself in language, consider anarchy an infinite demand. consider a world devoid of intimacy: we'd each be god or a rock

even resonance is deceptive.   I
catch   absent   voices,   echo's
immanence   magnetized   by
misdirection.   af-
ter   a   prolonged   wait,   hope
develops   an   immune
disorder,   manifests   only
digested   rage.   strah   krvari
i   kvari   mi   vreme: there   are
reasonable   fears,   such   as
stones in   *astonishment*

our hands catch fire waving goodbye; *nebo silazi u grad i obara reku bojama, ne boj se, ooze ooze*, my mental illness is no longer a contained field, feels like half-burnt coal, blows ripples on us, rips chrysalis, rips through the realism of ice: my body's water is turning inside out, struck perfusion. strident & no. OK unfolding and to what end. as if & nothing. wound up wrongly, insofar I. inasmuch I'm far from home. and far

your hands are the wolf howling counting absences.
your hands are the wolf howling counting absentees.
your hands are outside the image-controlled debris.
your hands are nonprofit ruptural intimacy.
your hands are bruised velvet.

the wolf is blowing up the moon, what voids
the universe abound. abides by, and binds
the story where the girl becomes the wolf.
your hands are meant to dress more than
the standardized wounds.

once eaten, a flower becomes part of the central nervous system.

meaning, not even anonymous memory is an innocent act.

as in: no person who had been touched is ever lost.

if you could taste moonlight: a thimble of sweat on a rose petal, mint. meanwhile the snow burns me, snow is tyranny over moving waters. snow continues to walk over water. I ask now leave to speak, I'm touched by light and a little jaundiced

someb
ody fi
xingm
ymout
hisho
lding
myface
inhis
hands.s
omebo
dyhold
ingmyf
aceinh
ismou
thisbr
eaking
myjaw.

may I be denied my body's monologue. may I worship the amnesiac muse. may the light unspool films on the surface of the river. may the hands, then, mother. be, unbind. may the howl lift the rapids. may the gods remember, rise the rotten apple to the mother. may the lively long. may I bite the arrow, coil the caul. may the mute direct the sentence, anoint the land captured before the photograph. may the eyes, then, mother. may our hands now empty god

to go on and live with. out.
outlive the with and. out
        love, love's
closing time in
the aftermath.
drenched I and sudden,
                        lilt,
lift me up in.
mer. in mur. mur per.
fumed. per form the alpha
bet and out. standing under.
I shook a center.
                the choice
the place has. has
taken place. the hole
begins   to breathe,
I. go my separate ways

fiction is engine of terrible precision. in a story, bodies of light ensue, break through condensation. my incantatory mind proves itself singularly impractical; incendiary, when I try to tell it all as-is: execute the sentence, exile the word. satisfy the need with stones.

somebody somewhere is always giving orders
neko negde daje naredbe   pogubne

                                              (gubiš me)

                                              (ubij me)

somebody somewhere is giving perilous   orders
(godine poludele zveče igračke)
nebo uvek daje naredbe nema   milosti

somewhere sky is always giving
orders. there's never been
mercy among the living. *jel*

možeš da zamisliš a fish that can swim through fire, svetlost
shining through light itself? *to si ti.*
that's you.

whose   daughter
  am I. scandalous

NIKOLINA LAZETIC was born in Sarajevo and grew up scattered along the Adriatic coast. she holds an MFA from Brown University and is currently a doctoral student at the University of Minnesota. she lives in Minneapolis—painting, blending scents.

www.ingramcontent.com/pod-product-compliance
Lightning Source LLC
LaVergne TN
LVHW032014070526
838202LV00059B/6451